COOKING WITH MATH!

MAKING SALADS WITH MATH!

By Santana Hunt

Gareth Stevens
PUBLISHING

Please visit our website, www.garethstevens.com. For a free color catalog of all our high-quality books, call toll free 1-800-542-2595 or fax 1-877-542-2596.

Library of Congress Cataloging-in-Publication Data

Names: Hunt, Santana.
Title: Making salads with math! / Santana Hunt.
Description: New York : Gareth Stevens Publishing, 2020. | Series: Cooking with math! | Includes glossary and index.
Identifiers: ISBN 9781538245705 (pbk.) | ISBN 9781538245729 (library bound) | ISBN 9781538245712 (6 pack)
Subjects: LCSH: Cooking–Mathematics–Juvenile literaure. | Mathematics–Juvenile literature. | Cooking–Juvenile literature. | Salads–Juvenile literature.
Classification: LCC TX652.5 H86 2020 | DDC 510–dc23

Published in 2020 by
Gareth Stevens Publishing
111 East 14th Street, Suite 349
New York, NY 10003

Designer: Katelyn E. Reynolds
Editor: Kate Mikoley

Photo credits: Cover, p. 1 The Magical Lab/Shutterstock.com; pp. 1-24 (gingham background) Mika Besfamilnaya/Shutterstock.com; pp. 1-24 (recipe background) A. Zhuravleva/Shutterstock.com; p. 5 Dragon Images/Shutterstock.com; p. 7 Ayanna Floyd-Wicks/Shutterstock.com; p. 11 © iStockphoto.com/EasyBuy4u; p. 12 rodrigobark/Shutterstock.com; p. 15 (cucumbers) Emily Li/Shutterstock.com; p. 15 (cherry tomatoes) kpboonjit/Shutterstock.com; p. 15 (peppers) bergamont/Shutterstock.com; p. 19 Africa Studio/Shutterstock.com; p. 20 RTimages/Shutterstock.com.

Printed in the United States of America

CPSIA compliance information: Batch #CW20GS: For further information contact Gareth Stevens, New York, New York at 1-800-542-2595.

CONTENTS

Boldface words appear in the glossary.

Superstar Salads

Salads are a tasty way to eat your fruits and veggies! In order to make a salad, you'll need to use math. Multiplication, subtraction, telling time, and measuring are just some of the math skills you can use in the kitchen!

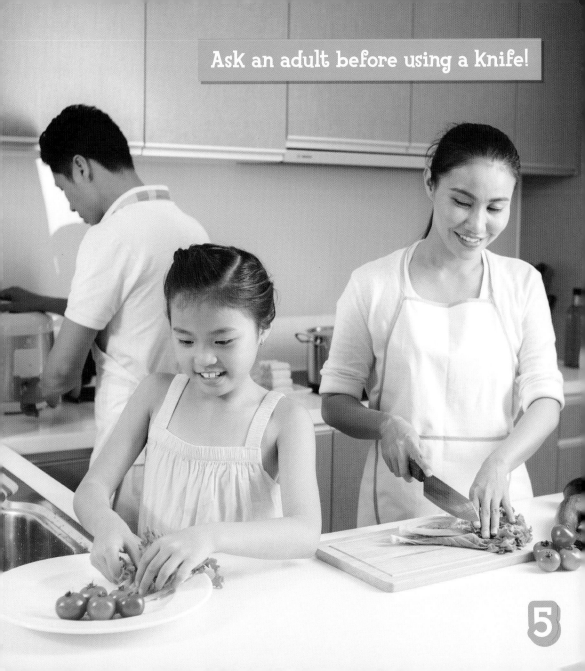

Ask an adult before using a knife!

5

Berry and Spinach Salad

A recipe tells you how to make a dish. It lists what **ingredients** you need and tells you how much of each to use. Sometimes **units**, such as cups and tablespoons, are used. Other times you may need to count the ingredients.

The berries in this salad make it taste sweet. If you think it might be too sweet, you can use less of some ingredients. If you use 4 fewer blueberries than the recipe calls for, how many would you use? Check your answer on page 22!

$$12 \text{ blueberries}$$
$$- 4 \text{ blueberries}$$
$$\text{? blueberries}$$

BERRY AND SPINACH SALAD

(makes about 2 servings)

Ingredients:

2 cups baby spinach
6 strawberries, sliced
12 blueberries
12 raspberries
1/8 cup goat cheese
3 tablespoons raspberry **vinaigrette**

Instructions:

1. In a large salad bowl, mix together all ingredients except the vinaigrette.

2. Mix in the raspberry vinaigrette. Another choice is to serve the vinaigrette on the side.

Three Bean Salad

Most grocery stores sell many kinds of salad dressing. But you don't have to stick to what's in the store. You can make your own dressing! Common ingredients in dressing are **vinegar** and olive oil, which is a yellowish oil made from small fruits called olives.

For the dressing in this bean salad, we need 1/2 teaspoon salt. You only have one measuring spoon. It measures 1/4 teaspoon. Can you still use this to measure the salt? How many times would you fill it?

THREE BEAN SALAD

(makes about 6 servings)

Ingredients:

1 can (15 ounces) Kidney beans
1 can (15 ounces) garbanzo beans
2 cups green beans, cooked
1/3 cup apple cider vinegar
1/4 cup olive oil
1/4 cup sugar
1/2 teaspoon salt
1/4 teaspoon pepper

Instructions:

1. Rinse and **drain** the Kidney beans and garbanzo beans.

2. Mix together the Kidney beans, garbanzo beans, and green beans in a bowl.

3. In another bowl, **whisk** the vinegar, olive oil, sugar, salt, and pepper.

4. Pour the dressing mixture over the bean mixture.

5. Refrigerate for at least 2 hours before serving.

13

Cheesy Veggie Salad

One great thing about salads is you can really make them your own! If you don't like an ingredient, you don't have to add it. If you really like an ingredient, you can add more of that ingredient.

cherry tomatoes

cucumbers

peppers

15

This recipe makes a great side salad. You could add beans or chicken to make it a meal. You could also add more tomatoes. If you wanted twice as many cherry tomatoes as the recipe calls for, how many would you need?

$$\begin{array}{r} 8 \text{ cherry tomatoes} \\ \times\ 2 \\ \hline ? \text{ cherry tomatoes} \end{array}$$

CHEESY VEGGIE SALAD

(makes about 2 servings)

Ingredients:

2 cups lettuce

8 cherry tomatoes

your choice chopped vegetables,
such as onions, carrots, cucumbers,
or peppers

1/4 cup shredded cheddar cheese

Instructions:

1. Have an adult help you cut the
   cherry tomatoes in half.

2. In a large salad bowl, mix together
   all ingredients.

3. Serve with your favorite dressing.

17

Fruit Salad

Sometimes recipes tell you how long it will take to make the dish, or they might tell you how long a certain step will take. A timer can help you keep track, but you should keep an eye on the clock too.

This salad tastes great cold. The recipe says it should go in the refrigerator for at least 15 minutes before you eat it. If you put it in the refrigerator at 4:10 p.m., what time can you take it out?
Use the clock to help you.

FRUIT SALAD

(makes about 4 servings)

Ingredients:

2 apples
2 cups watermelon, cut into **cubes**
8 strawberries
12 grapes
2 bananas

Instructions:

1. Have an adult help you cut the grapes and strawberries in half.

2. With the adult's help, cut the apples and bananas into bite-size pieces.

3. Mix all ingredients together in a bowl.

4. Put in the refrigerator for at least 15 minutes before serving.

Glossary

cube: a shape with six square sides

drain: to get rid of liquid by letting it flow out

ingredient: a food that is mixed with other foods

unit: an amount of length, weight, or volume that is used for counting or measuring

vinaigrette: a mixture of oil and vinegar that is often used as a salad dressing

vinegar: a sour liquid commonly used to flavor foods

whisk: to stir or mix food using a tool made of curved wire

Answer Key

p. 8 8 blueberries

p. 12 Yes; fill it twice.

p. 16 16 cherry tomatoes

p. 20 4:25 p.m.

For More Information

Books

Borgert-Spaniol, Megan. *Math You Can Munch.* Minneapolis, MN: Super Sandcastle, 2019.

Kuskowski, Alex. *Cool Sides & Salads: Easy & Fun Comfort Food.* Minneapolis, MN: Abdo Publishing, 2015.

Websites

2nd Grade Math
www.mathplayground.com/grade_2_games.html
Find math games here!

Cooking with Kids: How-to Videos
cookingwithkids.org/resources/how-to-videos-english/
This website has videos about topics such as how to make a salad and how to make salad dressing.

Index